playing monster :: seiche

.

1913 Press
www.1913press.org
1913press@gmail.com

Playing Monster :: Seiche
Copyright © 2017 by Diana Arterian

Manufactured in the oldest country in the world, the United States of America.

Many thanks to all the artists, from this century and the last, who made this project possible.

Founder & Editrice: Sandra Doller
Vice-Editor: Ben Doller
Managing Editrix: Adam Stutz
Editrix Team: Adam Bishop, Biswamit Dwibedy, Brianna Johnson, Emily Mernin, Yesenia Padilla, Leslie Patron
Designer: Joseph Kaplan
Layout: Diana Arterian

Cover art: *Entrance* © 2013 by Rebecca Chaperon
http://rebeccachaperon.com

ISBN: 978-0-9990049-0-6

Acknowledgements: Some of these poems have appeared (at times in earlier iterations) in *Anamesa*, *Boog City*, *Eleven Eleven*, *H_NGM_N*, *Iron Horse Literary Review*, *Roar*, *Sink Review*, *Two Serious Ladies*, *The Volta*, *Yew Journal*, and *Your Impossible Voice*. Many thanks to the editors and staff for their continual hard work in and for the literary community.

Disclaimer: While this work renders events from "real life," the author takes liberty with her representations of events, individuals, timelines, sources, etc., and makes no claim of factual accuracy in the work. Any similarity to any individuals other than members of the author's immediate family is coincidental.

playing

For Callie,
It's been so great
to get to know you
& for amazing work
these past years.
Thank you!
toDiana

monster ::

seiche

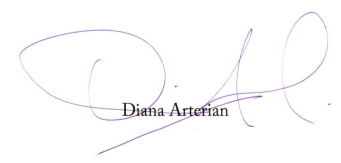

Diana Arterian

For my family

2.014   Objects contain the possibility
          of all situations.

ludwig wittgenstein

I stretch out on my bed and give in to the
"inner storm"; contrary to the Zen monk who
empties himself of his images, I let myself be
filled with them, I indulge their bitterness to
the full.

roland barthes

table of contents

110	one evening my father
111	my father discovered jesus
112	september 19, 1986
113	it is after church i will tell him
114	we find him in the parking lot
115	i tell him and he tells me
116	seconds later
117	he had wrenched their hands apart
118	we go to the police
119	or the man works a lock
120	my father, 1978
121	september 20, 1986
122	after my mother is granted
123	my father's wife
124	or the man silently
125	september 21, 1986
126	my father visits us frequently
127	i learn to keep information
128	after parent-teacher night
129	i try to shut my family up
130	he tells me in letters

prologue

found-text dated 1897 describing events
near my mother's home

ACCUSES HIMSELF OF MURDER.

He buried the body
exhumed it

threw it into
Onondaga Lake

after tying a stone
about the neck

driving us through a wood

my father makes out a stag
between pines in the mist

He pulls over for us to observe

I ask him to take a picture

No, he says
just look

and remember—remember
for the rest of your life

:: playing monster

interview

I want her to speak of it all

To liken herself
to that ancient noblewoman
who bore a child

on the battlefield

hoisted it in one arm

and wielded a sword
with the other

You make me feel like
I'm on my deathbed

Ask my sister—
her memory is better

:: playing monster

my mother, 1974

A young woman sits
on the train, briefcase
beside her, reading

A man walks over, quietly
opens his long coat to reveal
the nothing beneath

The woman looks up past
the desired location, into his eyes
Oh please—then back to her book

my aunt

Your mother was madly in love with your father when they were first together. She would call me during visits to his house and tell me how amazing he was. How he grew sunflowers. She doesn't tell you about that.

:: playing monster

seiche (/ˈseɪʃ/ *saysh*)

A phenomenon that occurs within a confined body of water such as a lake, sea, or pool. Once disturbed, the enclosed water may produce a "seiche" or standing wave that moves across its surface or, when below, between the warmer upper and colder lower layers. The wave does not break.

●

.

My mother is appointed
dean of a college

She buys a house
with a slate path

hires a man
to cultivate the yard

It is the most land
she has owned

A briar patch
berry trees

Wild peonies grow in the rough
of the yard next door

A friendly woman neighbor
appears one day—

invites my mother
to take peony cuttings

*Help yourself to whatever
you would like*

●

At twilight a man approaches
my mother's gardener

He is yelling at The Gardener
about cutting the peonies

trespassing on private property
The Gardener believes

The Neighbor
is drunk

But your wife
gave us permission—

My wife would never say that
She would never ever say that

The Gardener describes
the exchange to my mother

She grows worried
I'm not worried, he says

8

I have my shovel

:: seiche

arizona

It is a place where all that lives
has hardened and bristled
against the world without

It is a place where a man can beat his wife and daughter
and then his second wife, his son, and three daughters
then his third wife
without reckoning

I remember the red winds of a storm—
desert-shocking hail on a field

We are all pelted and bruised on our backs
wind herding us against fences

Through our cries I hear the laughter of my father
his face red, terrifying—

the storm the very cracks of his teeth

dear william, susannah, and diana,

While I was going through a drawer in my old dresser, I found a notebook in which over the course of about a month in 1986 I kept day-by-day lists of the good things, things that made me happy and such. These days were difficult for several reasons, including the fact your dad had been caught submitting fake grades to the law school. The question of what would happen to him was ongoing, and I was worried about the effect on you children as things appeared in newspapers and our neighbors found out.

Of course your little sister wasn't born yet, but I wanted to send you the things I felt good about that were about the three of you.

August 25, 1986
Diana wearing my underpants as a top.

William's hug and kiss before he went to sleep.

Susannah calling bras "brothers."

10

●

My mother has her property
surveyed to determine

where the line falls
The Neighbor posts

orange NO TRESPASSING signs
on trees facing her yard

They are bright enough to sight
over an acre away

She has The Gardener
plant a screen of bushes

so she can no longer
see the signs

from anywhere

11

my father and i are preparing a meal

He has to go outside, has
to tend to something

He instructs me not to touch
his ingredients

to continue slicing mushrooms

I do, wielding a knife
too large for my hand

When he returns, I watch
out of the corner of my eye

as he stops to scan
the items on the counter
with heavy pause—

he so certain
I have tampered with them

:: playing monster

august 26, 1986

Diana trying to put an old Band-Aid on my thumb, then kissing it.

William playing Name That Tune with me.

:: playing monster

●

My mother is at the office
The housecleaner pulls

into the driveway
spies a man drunk

moving down the back stone path
shouldering a large crossbow

The Housecleaner asks my mother
if she allows hunters on the property

though it is not the season
for bow hunting

:: seiche

my father is late

in sending his grades
for a class

The law school
pressures him

He turns them all in

including grades
for students who
have dropped the class

At last he confesses

he lost the finals
in South America

He is placed on forced leave
joins a local law firm
makes partner
stays on for five years

Tenured, he returns
to teaching

eventually makes
emeritus

:: playing monster

the cicadas emerge

leaving papery husks
on our citrus trees

These dark, silvery insects
frighten my older brother

Knowing this, my father
finds a dead one—

tells my brother
to hold it in his hand
for two minutes

My brother cannot do it

My father holds
his wrist

places the cicada
in his palm

The rest of him
shakes terribly

:: playing monster

Soon my mother spies
a raised stand for deer hunting

on The Neighbor's property
It is illegal to shoot game

so close to houses
She does not call the cops—

wants to exert
a quieter agency

To keep
very still

:: seiche

●

My mother rises early
to walk the dog

though The Dog can no longer
make it up the hill

It is winter
It is dark

Suddenly my mother sees
a man in clean camouflage

and a head lamp
in the road

It is not The Neighbor
It is a different man

She continues walking
They pass each other

Your dog is quiet today
he says

interlude

found-text dated 1877 describing events
near my mother's home

A MONSTER IN ONONDAGA LAKE.

he and his son were fishing
when surprised

by the sudden appearance
of a monster

It swam
along the surface

for several rods
then sank out of sight

my father

You don't know it now, but when you are older a light bulb will suddenly shine over your head and you will think, "Aha! My father was right."

he decides sugar is poison–

only puffed rice for cereal, though

our parents are always at the law school
when we eat breakfast

We all crawl onto the counter

to the sugar jar

spoon the whiteness, the whiteness
into our bowls

●

One morning my mother
wakes and looks out

her bedroom window
She sees tracks below

in the fresh snow across
most of yard

They are
a man's tracks

reeling

:: seiche

●

I am home for Christmas
Letting The Dog in

I spot boot prints
going around the house

which I track to the stairs
leading to the backdoor

The person paced at the base
of the flight, uncertain

My sister goes to inspect
They are dog tracks

The Dog went around back
With her bad hips

she can no longer climb stairs
She must have danced there

at the bottom

:: seiche

when my nanny marries

there are small sugared bells
on each tier of her cake

She gives a bell to my father
which he sets on his bureau

He discovers it later
chewed and broken
calls me into the room
the bell in his hand

I confess

He picks me up
by my shirt with
his teeth our eyes
so close he is shaking me
in the air dropping me

I make my way to
my mother
in the kitchen

24

I am shaking
She asks me what happened

I cannot speak

She takes me in her arms
where I shake

:: playing monster

my father apologizes

He mends his small holes
near the collar of my shirt

:: playing monster

Violence is the heart of it
A sure hand   all its capacity

Violence whistles sparks   The hand
clawing windfire

:: seiche

●

While walking The Dog
sometime later

my mother again
sees The Man

in camouflage
As they pass each other

he says, *This will be
a bad year for your college*

then turns around
passes her

trudges into a random yard
the pitch morning

:: seiche

august 28, 1986

Diana walking to pick up William—trying to carry a book and a jack-in-the-box.

Susannah playing imaginary games out loud.

Everyone seeming happy to see me when I get home.

:: playing monster

when my father hires our nanny

he tells my mother he knows her
through a connection in Mexico

Only later
when my mother learns
a little Spanish

and our nanny English

does my mother discover
he approached her
on the street

She becomes
like a second mother to us

She moves out when she marries
a white man I don't trust

who eventually nearly chokes her
to death before she leaves him

you want to know why

she stayed

but that
is a shapeless thing

It holds you in
when everything else
is howling

:: playing monster

Fire   The beauty is in
the blue of it   That dangerous shadow around her
barely visible   licking its fingers

:: seiche

●

The Dog starts suffering
from sporadic internal bleeds—

a fatal tumor
My mother must force-feed her

Our dog hates this
while loving my mother

The Dog is too ill
My mother has her put down

She regrets this
I should have let that dog decide

which heartbeat
would be her last

Some months later, lonely
my mother gets another dog

:: seiche

after a surgery in which

the doctors remove
a portion of his lung

my grandfather could not easily
climb a flight of stairs

When they were small
my mother and her sister
flew up the steps
to avoid his temper

But he followed, once

hounding my aunt to a room
My mother was there

Seeing her sister's fear
she said, *Strike me*

and he struck

august 30, 1986

Having 3 healthy children.

Having Diana come running to me when I got home.

:: playing monster

my father takes it upon himself

to treat our boils (the small buds

a hazard of spending all day
in swimsuits)

by piercing them
with clean needles
he keeps in a small
green prescription bottle

We lie on my brother's bed
while he sticks the pustules

I clench my teeth

He commends my bravery
I know it hurts like fire

perhaps this is why when

a man uncoils a paperclip
and uses it to gesture at me
I feel sick, must ask him to stop

:: playing monster

august 31, 1986

Diana lying flat on her back looking like a little frog.

:: playing monster

Years ago   a crushed toe flowing out
She laid me down   draped white cloth over it

Little ghost gaining color while she kissed
my wet cheeks
the blood coming up to meet her

:: seiche

long before he met my mother

my father went backpacking
through Peru

One night he was nearly asleep
on the ground when
a meteor shower
began to streak across the sky

He was terrified

He thought
it was the rapture

Though both are law professors
she always drives us to piano lessons
cooks dinner each night

He says nothing
about the meals

thanks God for dinner

my father takes my sister and I

to a fancy buffet one morning
where we pile our plates
with buttery eggs and fresh fruit

My father taps my shoulder
I look up to see his cheeks
stuffed with grapes, teeth
showing some, like a squirrel's
My sister and I laugh while
sliding grapes in our own cheeks
making faces, so we all laugh harder

The other adults stare
at the ruckus but
we keep on passing
the morning this way

:: playing monster

what does it say about someone when she is the favorite child of a sociopath?

(I hated
what he hated)

:: playing monster

interlude

found-text dated 1885 describing events
near my mother's home

A STEAMBOAT'S BOILER BURSTS.

two sharp reports were heard
the steamer instantly enveloped

in clouds of steam
The passengers saw a form

fling itself
out of a cloud

found writhing
scalded head to foot

In places the skin
rolled itself up

looked as if he had been
flayed alive

●

Someone sets a letter at each house
on my mother's street

that says she caused
a woman's suicide

Saying my mother did not renew
the woman's teaching contract

The Woman
was sick

The letter claims that is why
my mother did not renew her contract

The Woman killed herself by hoarding pills
while in the hospital

She killed herself
in the hospital

She left small children

44

The envelope bears no source
a single sheet within

One recipient places it
unopened

directly into a plastic bag
for the police

:: seiche

●

My mother tells the police
about The Woman

about The Neighbor
about The Man in camouflage

*I am not aware of anyone who
would send such a letter*, she says

After she hangs up
she turns to me

*Please don't
tell anyone*

:: seiche

my father and i

are sitting in a restaurant

I must say
The ant walks on the log
in Spanish

before I can eat

I cannot get beyond
La hormiga camina...

:: playing monster

there is no food or drink

allowed in bed

yet one night
my father finds my older sister
reading there with a glass of milk

He goes into a rage

throws himself
onto the bed
pounding his fists

into the mattress
around her, the milk

spilling everywhere

:: playing monster

What is a daughter then but clay eyes
ice   A witness twice over
The terror/father   Now faceless
fires advancing

:: seiche

in iowa

While visiting my father's parents
we are taken to a deer farm, promised
we are to bottle-feed fawns
pet the does

(all of which will someday
be mounted on walls)

While we walk among them
a stag suddenly charges
at my older sister

her back against a tree
the deer on its hind legs
front hooves tearing at the bark

My grandfather
my father
and the deer farmer
chuckle and watch

a woman we all call

Aunt Betty
is visiting
my grandmother

Aunt Betty
is suddenly sick

My father's mother
gives her a cooking pot

Aunt Betty vomits
into the pot

Once Aunt Betty
is composed

my grandmother
feeds the vomit

to the dogs

●

When someone
informed The Woman

that the college would not
renew her contract

The Woman howled
slipped from

her chair rolled
on the office floor

You're killing me
she said

I have cancer
she said

My mother worked to ensure the university
extended The Woman's health insurance

but before my mother told The Woman this
The Woman slipped letters

under everyone's door
in my mother's office

The notes said my mother
wanted her dead

:: seiche

●

A few weeks after
the anonymous notes

to her neighbors
my mother gets a letter

"Murderer"—
that's how it started

she tells me
I just want it to stop

:: seiche

●

The police send a patrol car
through the neighborhood

now and then
My mother's friend

convinces her to hire
a private detective

The Detective is the only reason
the cops probe deeper

The Detective hounds them
He tells them this is urgent

:: seiche

●

My sister is home
She calls me

Something is wrong, she says
I tell her everything I know

We worry aloud
Our mother tells us nothing

This is knowledge
by chance

interlude

found-text dated 1884 describing events
near my mother's home

OPENING INDIAN BURIAL GROUND.

Laborers were leveling
a mound of earth

on the shores
of Onondaga Lake

came upon a pile of skulls
and skeletons

The mound a graveyard
for the Onondaga

The bodies crumbled to dust
being exposed to air

The archeologists drilled
without discovering anything

canoeing

with my grandfather
and his friend

I am talking
loudly

to the other person
in the boat

My grandfather
tells me
Be quiet—you
are scaring
the fish

As a baby I suffered
from a severe
ear infection
so I often speak
too loudly

He warns me
again
to quiet down

I don't

:: playing monster

I feel
the sharp
whack of the paddle just
above the healed ear

:: playing monster

my grandfather

slaps my brother
across the face
in front of my mother

She grabs him
Don't you ever
touch my son again

september 3, 1986

William drawing a rattlesnake on my mom's thank you note.

:: playing monster

my maternal grandmother dies

the day before I turn three
My mother gets the phone call
while my parents are hosting a dinner

She does not let herself cry
until the guests leave

My father doesn't allow us
to attend the funeral

He tells my mother
she can bring nothing home
from my grandmother's house

Later she tells me
When I think about
what I left on that street corner

it makes me
want to scream

a year later we become

Corey, the infant

Diana, four years old

Susannah, seven

and William, nine

:: playing monster

When a child   I imagined her arms
Arms wind around her now
fleshy ribbons   coiling around
I feel them slow   like snakes

:: seiche

●

I knew this woman
had a history

of illness
but not

mental illness
Not that she had tried

to kill herself
several times

I don't think
she really meant

to kill herself
She was in a hospital

She was being discharged
that day

She probably thought
she would be saved

64

I feel guilty
about many things in life

:: seiche

but I know
I didn't kill

that woman

:: seiche

one night my father calls the house

from South America

I pick up the phone

He wants to talk to Corey

I say she is sleeping
He tells me to rouse her

I ask my mother

Tell him she is asleep—I said
you can't wake her

I go back to the phone
and my mother hears
as I mimic the voice
of my toddler sister

as if he could reach
through the phone

and grab me
when I didn't obey

:: playing monster

september 6, 1986

Diana singing along with me at bedtime.

:: playing monster

my mother surprises us one easter–

baskets brimming
with chocolates though
candy is not allowed

We find the baskets
while it is still dark

A few minutes later
my father enters our room
takes the baskets away

tells us our mother
is the Easter Bunny
and exits

While we eat
what we stashed
under our pillows
our parents fight

though we never
hear these fights

It is during this argument
that my mother decides
he must leave—

when he knocks her
onto the bed and puts

:: playing monster

his hand over
her mouth

to silence her

She sleeps on the couch
for nearly a year

but it is only
when she agrees to pay
fifty thousand dollars
of his debt
that he leaves
for good

:: playing monster

We are all home
for Christmas again

One morning
my mother announces

she has an appointment
and leaves

Later she tells me
in private

she had gone
to the police station

Looked at mug shots
Apparently The Woman

had a brother
who was a policeman

He was discharged
for some reason

The police seem to think
he is their best bet

The Man in camouflage
had a goatee

:: seiche

So did
The Woman's brother

But I couldn't tell
for sure

:: seiche

I spend a winter Sunday alone
the way I imagine

my mother does
I walk the new dog up the hill

I read for most of the day
Listen to the house tick

Before bed
I take The Dog out again

then stand and watch
as she barks at the trees

in the dark yard

:: seiche

It does not gather up   plunge
It may be slow   like a dance
as a heartbeat   slower

:: seiche

interlude

found-text dated 1879 describing events
near my mother's home

DROWNED IN ONONDAGA LAKE.

Until a late hour
efforts were made

by means of grappling hooks
to recover the bodies

Things go calm
and quiet

stay that way

:: seiche

The *puh* of something catching   Flamesounds
Flags in quick wind   Whatever is caught
untwists   cracks open further
tiny red fingers combing through the embers   And what
of what stays locked shut?

when it nears time

to go to his house
my older brother and sister cry

wring their little hands

I tell them
It's only three days
It's only three days

:: playing monster

i am at my father's house

I have upset him
We are standing
a few feet apart

My bottom lip
is trembling

I cannot stop it

He stares at me
He does not break

:: playing monster

when at his house

we are not allowed
to call my mother

My older siblings call her
while hiding under their beds

They leave her voicemails
when she is still at work

Mommy I hate this
Mommy please

september 9, 1986

Susannah's picture home from school "I like my house, I don't want to move."

A triple hug from the kids for my birthday.

my father and i stand

in front of his bathroom mirror

He is shaving with his antique kit
He stops, looks at me
in the mirror

His child

He says, *If anyone*
ever steals you away
poke out
the man's eye

I can run, I say—

No—take your finger
and get it into his socket
behind the eye

then pull forward

:: playing monster

my aunt and her family fly out

for Christmas   the first
without my father there

Late Christmas Eve while she
and my mother quietly set
presents under the tree
his headlights move
over them as he pulls
into the driveway

They don't move

He idles there, lights
on them a long while

then pushes
back into the night

:: playing monster

Things go calm
and quiet

Or my mother
lets The Dog out

one night
Minutes later she calls

and calls through
cupped hands

The Dog
never returns

:: seiche

●

My mother opens
the front door

The Dog is there
gutted entrails

splayed out
like a fan

A gift

:: seiche

●

Or my mother is out back
with The Dog

It is late
The Dog thirty feet away

My mother hears
a sharp *thew*

then a thin whistle
The Dog collapses

a crossbow's feathered bolt
lodged in her breast

:: seiche

●

Or things go calm
and quiet

stay that way

:: seiche

the dentist convinces my father

that I should have eight baby teeth
pulled at once

The dentist gives me eight shots
some in my palate
which is very painful

After he begins to pull I lose blood
see cartoons playing in my eyes
and black out

My dad wakes me, tells me
it is time to go to school
but I am so tired
I try to lay down on a bench
in the office as we leave
I pass out in his car

Instead of school he takes me
to my mother's house
She had no knowledge
of my appointment
the dentist's plan

That night at her house I get $20
from the tooth fairy, feel rich

It takes the adult teeth years
to fill the gaps

september 10, 1986

Diana's joke, "Where are you going my Diana, Diana?"
"Go to sleep."

after my father is ordered

by a judge to pay child support
he sits us down
He tells us our mother
is Hitler

when staying with my father

my brother passes
my mother's house
on the way to middle school

He visits her, secretly

During one of their visits
she sees visible bruises

Normally my father struck us
with an intelligence
leaving nothing

My mother tells William
to show the bruises
at school

The counselor
calls my father's house that night
to talk to my brother

My father listens in

learns
from this mistake

:: playing monster

september 13, 1986

*William saying if he had one wish he'd make me the longest
living woman in the world and him the longest living boy.*

:: playing monster

my older sister

walks to my mother's house
after softball practice

She is hysterical

My father
held a broken spoon
to her neck
pressed it

My mother urges her
to stay—*No I have
to go back*

*I can't let him
hurt the others*

soon my older sister

tells my father she
will not be going
to his house anymore

I am in that room when she tells him

Every thing in it
humming

:: playing monster

september 15, 1986

Going to the grocery store with Susannah, feeling lucky to have her.

:: playing monster

years later my sister says

You all just stood there
saying nothing

:: playing monster

i start having the fantasy

of getting to eye level
with my father

tearing at his face
until it is bloody and raw

leaving his lower lids
hanging loose

:: playing monster

september 16, 1986

Listening to the children describe the baby bird they tried to save.

Watching Diana tap her feet after church and laugh when I tap mine and on and on.

:: playing monster

To contain this fire   dam it up
Can I open myself   river it in

:: seiche

●

Or The Housecleaner comes
sees my mother's car

She calls out to her
goes up the stairs

to my mother's room
My mother is in bed

She is not moving

:: seiche

Or my mother is walking The Dog
early in the morning

She hears footsteps
They break into a run

She turns
The Man reaches her

As they collapse onto salted blacktop
she draws a small hidden blade

:: seiche

Or things go calm
and quiet

:: seiche

Or my mother goes to work
The Woman is sitting

in my mother's office chair
She laughs as my mother blanches

You thought I was dead, she says

●

Or I get a letter
I track down its author

I stand in a dark corner
of his home

for hours
watching the light shift

When he enters
I draw a gun

shoot him cleanly
between the eyes

●

Or I am in the backyard
Suddenly The Neighbor's Wife

is beside me
clutching peonies

She knocks me down
rips the petals

shoves them
in my throat

then covers my eyes
with cool eel grass

lays me out
on the calm snow

:: seiche

●

Or things go quiet

stay that way

:: seiche

interlude

found-text dated 1882 describing events
near my mother's home

SHOOTING HIS MISTRESS AND HIMSELF.

became jealous
went with

the avowed purpose
of killing her

he shot the girl
fled seeking refuge

in the house of his father
on Onondaga Lake

Upon reaching his bedroom

my mother goes to the gym

every morning before dawn

I am always up
when she leaves

I start to worry
she will die in a crash

I sit by the door
every morning
until I hear the garage open

She catches me

She explains
the drive is short
there is no one on the road

The feeling persists

my younger sister

People don't get it—he wasn't a drunk, he wasn't a deadbeat, he didn't abandon us. They don't understand why we don't talk to him. A friend recently told me most people just thought he was dead.

:: playing monster

i am in the backseat

of my father's car

He is driving
with his soon-to-be
third wife
in the passenger's seat

We are silent

She is looking out
at the neighborhood

She says, *All the
black people
have just ruined
this place*

He laughs it off

I feel my hair
rise against her

:: playing monster

one evening my father

decides to teach
my younger sister
then six
how to do
a proper pushup

He readjusts her
roughly
several times

until her back
is like a little plank

her arms
can barely hold her

:: playing monster

my father discovered jesus

in Saudi Arabia

He was a teenager—
his father finding
oil fields there

*I floated home
from church that day*
he writes

in a letter
addressed to me
when I am near the age
of his rebirth

september 19, 1986

Having a long talk with Susannah.

Diana just running around.

:: playing monster

it is after church i will tell him

I have decided my father
will not take me to buy a gift
for my friend's birthday
My mother will

I must tell him this

I grow very afraid

My older sister coaches me
We play hooky from Sunday school

I cry for two hours

My sister tells me I have eyes
like my grandfather's
the one person we know
who scares my father

Look scary—steel eyes
Grandpa eyes

We will be in public

Nothing will happen

She will be there
with me

we find him in the parking lot

My mother is parked far away

He sees her

I tell him
I must tell him something
He tells Susannah to leave

She says no

He tells her again, differently

She leaves

:: playing monster

i tell him and he tells me

I am being ridiculous
but lets me go

I get in my mother's car

We wait for Susannah
who is still inside
with Corey

The church door to the parking lot
opens I see
Susannah's hand

I hear her scream

The hand is gone
The door slams shut

I am in the car
I am the blood in my ears
I am stone

seconds later

Susannah emerges

Crying, she says she has to go
back into the church

Corey is in the church
She has to get Corey

We try to stop her

She runs back in
and staggers out
carrying Corey
who is also crying

a scratch on her heel—
my father was so close
his shoe caught
the skin

he had wrenched their hands apart

grabbed Susannah
by the shoulders

slammed her against
the wall over and again

Why are you taking her away
from me why are you taking
her away

we go to the police

They do nothing

Just as we
have always feared

:: playing monster

●

Or The Man works a lock
to the house

as a patrol car eases by
The Man runs

Police pursue him on foot
through thickets

over fences
frozen ponds

They run for hours
Give up

A hunter finds
The Man's body

weeks later
frozen in the woods

my father, 1978

My father and mother
are walking together
in Manhattan
My father visiting
from Iowa

A man approaches them
demands all their money

He sees my father's
pocket watch—a gift
from my grandmother

He tells my father
to give him the watch

My father says no

The man
again demands
the watch

He is again
denied

The man
walks
away

september 20, 1986

Diana covering her face with a shirt and playing monster.

:: playing monster

after my mother is granted

full custody
I stop crying completely

I do not cry
for four years

My siblings tell me
I am a robot

with a heart of stone

:: playing monster

my father's wife

begins to call the house
to talk to my mother

She is often crying

telling my mother
the horrible things
he says and does

She always punctuates
these talks with
But he loves me so
I know I
can change him

The calls continue
at all times of day
and night

One evening
my mother
tells her she is with

the children
we are eating dinner
and she is going

to hang up
now

:: playing monster

●

Or The Man silently
picks the lock

He removes his shoes
ascends the stairs

toe-heel
No sound

He lies in bed
next to my mother

He takes in
a long breath

removes a razor
from a small box—

his wrists
two quick blooms

124

:: seiche

september 21, 1986

The musical the children put on.

Diana with a ponytail and dress saying goodbye to me.

:: playing monster

my father visits us frequently

and unannounced

Legally, he cannot enter the house

He knocks: *tap*—
tap-tap tap—*tap-tap-tap*

I often hide in the bathroom
until he leaves

Or I go out as we all
usually do
one by one

He sits on the porch
and talks to us

We look down
answer his questions
the air sucked away

One day I call out
from the hallway

I tell him I will not sit with him

Then I retreat to where
he cannot go
or see

:: playing monster

I learn to keep information

from my father's parents
despite my being close to them
as a child

I stop sending school pictures
making phone calls

I know
they turn everything
over to him

after a parent-teacher night

my very pregnant
middle school teacher
tells me how much
she loves my dad

How he is very attractive

I tell her he is sixty, knowing
she must be half this age

She says he is charming

I realize he is
seen this way

i try to shut my family up

when they talk about him—

he is always about power

and I want to allow him
none of it

I think of my aunt, saying

You all talk about him a lot—
it's like he's always in the room

he tells me in letters

that I need
to forgive him

*The anger
will poison
your heart*

He doesn't know
I abandoned
the anger

It was more
than he deserved

despite our moving

far away
my father attends
my high school graduation

He parks and waits

for us to return from dinner
to knock and cause

the old panic

in the new
safe place

september 22, 1986

The girls jumping to "Yellow Dog Dingo."

while in college

my older sister
begins to have flashbacks

She remembers
being in my father's house
late at night

alone with him

What happened next
is too terrible
to remember

She remembers
the dread, she says

and that is enough

september 23, 1986

Picking up Susannah from Kindergarten and having her look neat including the flower still in her hair.

:: playing monster

later my mother tells me

that during the divorce
the judge took her
aside and told her
she was asking
for a lot

Still, he awarded her
most of it

My father didn't pay

My mother sued, asked
that the money
be drawn directly
from his paychecks

The judge
obliged her request

in full capital letters

in the order

:: playing monster

my mother

He actually thought he would win after the same judge ordered he pay child support in the first case. That's how nuts he was. He thought he didn't have to pay a dime of support for his four children.

:: playing monster

a few law students

were externing
at the courthouse
at the time

They sat in the back
of the courtroom

through the whole
of the divorce proceedings

My mother is relieved
she listened to her lawyer—
did not speak of the abuse

(no police reports
or physical evidence
make it thin)

At least
she preserved some
small piece of privacy

june 15, 2007

It was after this date
that my mother

felt she could die

For on this day
her youngest child
became a legal adult

and only then
could she be absolutely sure
none of her children

would be given somehow
back to him

I wish she were something I could touch
like a stone   Instead of a burning
twisting around us

:: seiche

i ask my mother

about the journal entries—
all recorded events
I don't remember

They are daily denials
aren't they?

Her therapist at the time told her
she was too negative
about her life

This was an assignment

i see i have made

my mother think
of it all
too much

You see me
as the victim, she says

but maybe I'm not

:: playing monster

●

Or things go calm
and quiet

stay that way

:: seiche

september 25, 1986

William asking me what my favorite thing about him was and telling him it was his soul. Him saying, "I thought it was my sense of humor."

:: playing monster

we decide the worst part

of my brother's wedding
is not my father being invited

but rather
that when my younger sister
voices our distress
to women who say

You all need to grow up

He is your father, you know

:: playing monster

as a teenager

I got letters
from my real father

The father I wish
I had

They were full of love
and remorse

My real father exists
from a phantom hand

So I hold emptiness

But it is *my* void—
my own

:: playing monster

one day my younger sister

makes a passing remark
about my father
sleeping with other women
while married to my mother

This is a surprise to me

She assures me it is true—

motel receipts
in his shirt pocket

my younger sister

has become a container of information
about my parents' marriage

This is likely due
to her curiosity

being alone in the house
while my mother
was away on business
for days on end

She found and read
my mother's diaries
which go back
years and years

to when my brother
was a baby

and even before

according to my sister

my mother wrote
that she realized
my father didn't love her
on their wedding day

She wrote she could not
be with him for long
after my brother
was born

Grief rises in me
rises and pulls
itself forward

148

september 26, 1986

Susannah at ballet class.

Diana with her hair in a ponytail.

William's enthusiasm.

Loving my children.

Feeling they love me back.

:: playing monster

●

Or I take The Dog
to Onondaga Lake

It is deserted
A building across

pumps out thin clouds
against the sun

A sharp wind
off the water

I walk in
past the icy fringe

I dredge up the bodies
all the bone clusters

that line the bottom
Gather them in my arms

Take them to the house
Shove them upright

into the ground
one by one

:: seiche

I build a knobby fence with them
This makes it

stop

:: seiche

Mourning dove calling on my mother's roof   *Like Arizona*
our old home   We sit   close our eyes
feel fire-oven heat   olive leaves
our then-threat of my father   real but known

apparently my namesake

is a Mexican painter
he dated briefly

My mother didn't know this
until they bought a painting
hung it on their wall

He said it reminded him
of someone

:: playing monster

a person with knowledge

and a full account of the story
thinks it likely that as a child
my father endured sexual violence

I know the victim-
to-perpetrator arc well

(It is one I fear, trailing me—
my tired shadow)

I never thought this haunting his

He instead sick from no source

Born to harm

So this revelation
it stops me dead
in my tracks a while

i try hard

to become porcelain

I go out with friends

press my hands
on my face all night

Just a heavy coat
on a thin fucking hanger

i learn that the more

one revisits a memory
the more it changes

My remembrance
of the day at church

Me, who just stared

at the door

behind which everything
took place

a man comes into

the pizza place where I work

asks me
to fill a cup
with boiling water

I know
he will use this

as a weapon on me

Five minutes later
he returns
with the cup

now asking
for cold water

I look in:
a baby's bottle

:: playing monster

two men yelling

Broad daylight, the shouts
pushed to a point

A current of fear
goes through me

*What? They
are only fighting*

My childhood was
so different

In mine—
you see a battle
but cannot hear it

The smoke plumes—
silence

●

I call my mother
I don't tell my mother

what I have tried to write about
but I can barely touch—

her
her hair

her hands
lips

How I cannot stand close
looking out with her

I tell her I am writing about
Onondaga Lake

But Diana, she says
you haven't even been there

:: seiche

walking to my apartment late at night

the smallest movement
provokes a wave of fear—

a plastic bag blowing by

a cat moving across a fence

But it is also
the non-moving

Light hitting a car seat
is suddenly a man's face
staring at me

Then it isn't

a professor asks

what we associate
with nighttime

I say it is a time
when we, as animals
are most unsafe

Something to be survived—
as in: *She won't make it
through the night*

:: playing monster

i start to worry

about accidentally
killing
anything alive

:: playing monster

eating dinner

a friend asks how I am

I tell him I served
a customer soda from
the fountain that day and

before placing a cap over
the lip of the cup I looked

down at the hiss of bubbles
so tight and continuous
and feverish I

was overwhelmed and
filled with dread—*Diana, you
need help*

eventually a friend

gives me a Xanax

That night, alone
the window slams shut

I feel nothing

Incredible

no doctors

will prescribe me Xanax

One gives me
something else

It makes me jumpy—
a certain turn of my head
provokes the feeling
of metal moving on metal

I see a psychiatrist
she says Xanax is addictive

I get seven pills
out of her

My younger sister
gives me all of her Xanax

I take whole pills
fall asleep while driving

sitting in a hammock

in a quiet place
reading Sappho

I decide if reality isn't *true*
then so what—it's
all I have

:: playing monster

nearly asleep

I hear a man's voice

shouting in my mind

The heater clicks off—
the voice stops

:: playing monster

i ask my mother

if there is anything else
I should know

She says, *I'm sure
there is but
you're not going
to know it*

*Just say
"My mother
won't tell me
everything"*

:: playing monster

notes

All found-text pieces are from unattributed articles published by *The New York Times* and are in the public domain.

My mother's diary entries are included with permission.

gratitude to

my mother, brother, and sisters for answering all the difficult questions I needed to ask. Your enduring support of me, of each other, is beyond healing. This is for you.

ali-reza for being there while I dealt with the answers, and beyond.

maggie nelson for being a guiding light during this book's dark beginnings and development—and for one of its titles.

sarah vap, master weaver, for helping me finish what I started.

those who read and prodded: Todd Fredson, Carmen Giménez Smith, Brenda Hillman, Lily Hoang, Jen Hofer, Christine Kanownik, Nicholas Katzban, Ruth Madievsky, Susan McCabe, Alice Notley, Janet Sarbanes, Corinna McClanahan Schroeder, David St. John, Mathias Viegner, Simone White, and Joseph P. Wood.

the staff, faculty, and my peers at the University of Southern California PhD in Literature & Creative Writing Program and the CalArts MFA in Critical Studies Program who are too many to name yet have supported me and my work far beyond reading and editing. Also to Austin Beutner and Virginia Beutner of the CalArts Board for their generosity, and the Caldera Arts Center Residency staff and board for the providing funds, time, and space.

my book makers: the marvelous editors and staff at 1913 Press for their effusive support, and Joseph Kaplan for designing with such care and beauty.

diana arterian is the author of the chapbooks *Death Centos* (Ugly Duckling Presse), *With Lightness & Darkness and Other Brief Pieces* (Essay Press), and co-editor of *Among Margins: Critical & Lyrical Writing on Aesthetics* (Ricochet). A Poetry Editor at Noemi Press, her creative work has been recognized with fellowships from the Banff Centre, Caldera, Vermont Studio Center, and Yaddo. Her poetry, essays, and translations have appeared in *Asymptote*, *BOMB*, *Black Warrior Review*, *Boston Review*, *Denver Quarterly*, and *Los Angeles Review of Books*, among others. This is her first full-length poetry collection.

Born and raised in Arizona, she currently resides in Los Angeles where she is a doctoral candidate in Literature & Creative Writing at the University of Southern California.

titles from 1913 press

forthcoming

Lucy 72 by Ronaldo V. Wilson

Umbilical Hospital by Vi Khi Nao

Dreaming of Ramadi in Detroit by Aisha Sabatini Sloan (selected by

Maggie Nelson)

On Some HispanoLuso Miniaturists by Mark Faunlagui (selected by Ruth

Ellen Kocher)

Conversations Over Stolen Food by Jon Cotner & Andy Fitch

Old Cat Lady: A Love Story in Possibilities by Lily Hoang

Strong Suits, Brad Flis

Hg, the liquid by Ward Tietz

1913 titles are distributed by Small Press Distribution: www.spdbooks.org